Meet this small group of Pelicans, November 1, 2019. They were hanging out on a small "island" of dirt, at the Audubon Riverlands Center, in West Alton, MO. I have numbered them to make it easier to follow the story.

We don't know if this pelican is a boy or girl. Only THEY know that.
We will call it a girl though. She is just relaxing at the moment.
2

Big yawn starting. Pelicans have a BIG mouth.
It's called a POUCH. It's used for catching fish.

3

She is facing the sun and is puffing air into her pouch so it will get more fresh air and sunshine on it.

Putting a close up in here for you to get a better loook at her beak.

Tilting her head WAY back.

13

She is finishing her yawn. It took about seven seconds!!!!

As you can see, her beak is still fluffed up a litttle.

Ok, so now we are going to watch the interaction between #2 and #4. There is not much room on this "island" and # 4 does not have room to spread out her wings. while she is preening. (cleaning her feathers).

4
2
Pelican #2 is very engaged in her preening efforts,
not noticing the wing dilemma of her island mate #4.

Aha!! #4 has stepped away a little so she can raise her other wing.
Her right foot is up just a bit while she is moving.

Her left foot is up and she's moving closer to #2.

Well, she is saying something.
Probably "one of has to move and it's not going to be me!!!!"

Well, we will see.

#2 is beginning a move.

She is definately moving. It looks confusing to me
but I am sure THEY know what they are doing!!

I wonder how far she will go. The island is not very big.

25

Almost there I think.

27

It looks like she has about 50 black feathers!

She's balancing herself and getting settled into her spot.

By the way. Did you notice this extra growth on her right ankle?
I just noticed that. Did you?

Pretty well all stretched out and getting ready
to clean her feathers again.

She's finished with cleaning her feathers,
and he is ready to go somewhere.

36

Now that she has moved to the front of the group,
she is taking off. Going somewhere else.

Probably going to visit some other friends.

Goodbye for now!.

White American Pelican information:

Scientific name:
Kingdom: Animalia
hylum: Chordata
Class: Aves
Order: Pelecaniformes
Family: Pelecanidae
Genus: Pelecanus
Species: Pelecanus erythrorhynchos

Length: About 50-70 inches
Beak :   11.3-15.2 Long
Wing span: 95-120 inches
Weight: 11-20 pounds

American White Pelicans migrate twice a year. In the winter they are on the Gulf Coast, California and Mexico. In the spring they migrate to their summer nesting areas in the Great Plains and the Great Basin. First between February to March and again from October to November.

The Pelicans in this book were at the
Audubon Center at Riverlands
301 Riverlands Way,
 West Alton, MO

CATS
Lexi My Cat
Cat Portraits
Cats Speak

DOGS
Dogs of Circle Lake
Dog Portraits
Barnhunt Dogs
Seasoned Dogs
With Bright Shiny Facces

VARIETY
What are they thinking?
Paws on a Line
Animals Dont Wear Lipstick
Subliminal Nuances of-
Animal Behavior

CARTOON COLORING Books
Tra La La
Time to Smell the Flowers
A-Z Capital Letters
a-z-lower case letters

BONOBO BOOKS
I'm Lucy: A Day in the Life of a
Young Bonobo
Is Lucy Singing?
Grooming Bonobos: -
Lucy Loves it
Bonobo Lucy Grows Up
Bonobo Lucy and her Baby Yulli

Bonobo Empathy Books
Insides Out
You Scared Me.
I'm Different-You're Different

Birds
Go Fish
We're Collegial Birds
Trumpeter Swans
Trumpeter Swans Discussion
Happy Gulls

Books by Marian Brickner